STICKER ROAD TRIP

50

STATES

WRITTEN BY
COURTNEY ACAMPORA

ILLUSTRATED BY
SARA LYNN CRAMB

Silver Dolphin

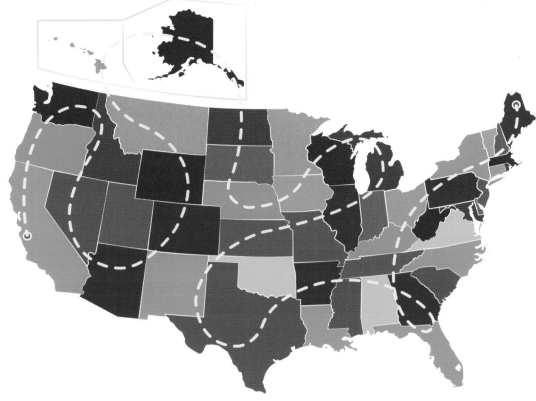

Silver Dolphin Books

An imprint of Printers Row Publishing Group
10350 Barnes Canyon Road, Suite 100, San Diego, CA 92121
www.silverdolphinbooks.com

Printers Row Publishing Group is a division of Readerlink Distribution Services, LLC.
The Silver Dolphin Books name and logo are trademarks of Readerlink Distribution Services, LLC.

Written by Courtney Acampora
Designed and illustrated by Sara Lynn Cramb

ISBN: 978-1-62686-706-2

Manufactured, printed, and assembled in Shenzhen, China.
First Printing, January 2016.

20 19 18 17 16   1 2 3 4 5

TABLE OF CONTENTS

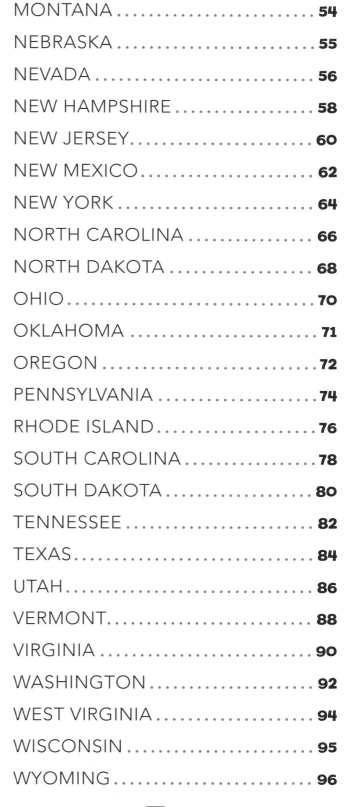

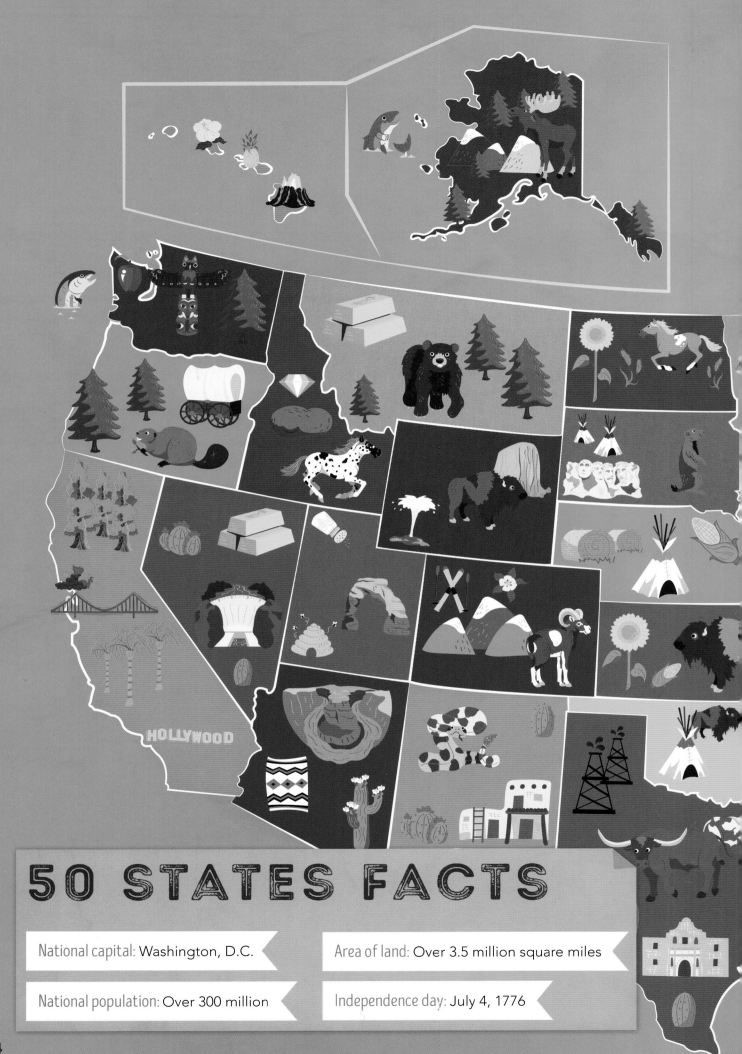

50 STATES FACTS

National capital: Washington, D.C.

Area of land: Over 3.5 million square miles

National population: Over 300 million

Independence day: July 4, 1776

Welcome to the 50 states!

The United States of America is one nation made up of 50 individual states, and each state is as special as the people that live in our amazing country. Whether it's mile-high mountains or white sandy beaches, some of the most beautiful scenery in the world is found right here. Get ready for a trip across the 50 states to learn about what makes each state so special.

United States of America
July 4, 1776

Washington, D.C.

5

ALABAMA

Use your stickers to fill in Alabama's famous landmarks!

Alabama's official **state insect** is the MONARCH BUTTERFLY. The monarch butterfly is a **long-distance migrator**, fluttering nearly 2,500 miles to warmer climates in the winter.

● Huntsville

Magnolia, Alabama, has many **waterways**. It is the only city in the United States where all MAIL is **delivered by boat**!

● Magnolia

☆ MONTGOMERY

● Andalusia

MISSISSIPPI

The WORLD CHAMPIONSHIP DOMINO TOURNAMENT is held in **Andalusia, Alabama**. But it is against the law to play dominoes anywhere in Alabama on Sundays.

LOUISIANA

GULF OF MEXICO

6

Alabama, known as the "Heart of Dixie," is located in the southeastern United States. The name "Alabama" comes from a group of Native Americans who once lived there—the Alibamu. Alabama is home to green rolling plains, and rivers and streams that flow into the Gulf of Mexico.

Alabama
22nd state
December 14, 1819

NORTH CAROLINA

SOUTH CAROLINA

ATLANTIC OCEAN

GEORGIA

FLORIDA

The FIRST ROCKET made to put humans on the Moon was built in **Huntsville, Alabama**.

It's against the law in Alabama to wear a fake MUSTACHE to church just to make people laugh.

STATE FACTS

Nickname: The Heart of Dixie ♥

State Capital: Montgomery ★

Date of Statehood: December 14, 1819, the 22nd state

State Bird: Yellowhammer

State Mammal: Black Bear

State Flower: Camellia

Use your stickers to fill in Alaska's famous landmarks!

Alaska has over 100 **VOLCANOES** that have been active the past **two million years**! **Eighty percent of the volcanoes** in the United States are found in Alaska.

Nome

Anchorage

PACIFIC OCEAN

Every winter, in Alaska's **IDITAROD SLED DOG RACE**, mushers and teams of **sixteen dogs** race from **Anchorage to Nome**. The trek over the snow is often in freezing temperatures and blizzard conditions, and **can take between eight and fifteen days**.

There is no way to drive into **Juneau**, Alaska's capital. You can only get there by **PLANE** or ferry.

Alaska, located in the north and separate from the rest of the states, was the second-to-last state added to the country. The name "Alaska" derives from the native Aleut word "aleyska," which means "great land." Because it is located so far north where it is colder, Alaska is home to many large glaciers. Bering Glacier is the largest, measuring 2,250 square miles! During the cold, dark winter the Northern Lights are visible—bright, colorful, glowing bands of light across the sky.

Alaska
49th state
January 3, 1959

A lot of Alaska is covered in **GLACIERS**. A glacier is a large, moving **ice mass**. Alaska has more than **100,000 glaciers**!

CANADA

When **GOLD** was discovered in Alaska in 1898, over **30,000 people** flocked to the area. Gold is also Alaska's **state mineral**.

JUNEAU

STATE FACTS

Nickname: The Last Frontier

State Capital: Juneau

Date of Statehood: January 3, 1959, the 49th state

State Bird: Willow Ptarmigan

State Mammal: Moose

State Flower: Forget-Me-Not

ARIZONA

Use your stickers to fill in Arizona's famous landmarks!

Over **millions of years**, the **Colorado River** has carved its way through layers of rock to form Arizona's **GRAND CANYON**. What's left behind are striking **layers of colored rock** nearly a mile deep.

NEVADA

UTAH

Winslow

Lake Havasu City

CALIFORNIA

PHOENIX

Sonoran Desert

MEXICO

The original **LONDON BRIDGE** was built in England in 1831, taken apart in 1967, and reconstructed in **Lake Havasu City, Arizona**, in 1971.

SAGUARO CACTI are only found in the Sonoran Desert. The saguaro is the **largest cactus** in the United States and can live to be up to **200 years old**!

Arizona, the 48th state, has some of the most diverse geography and weather in the United States. It has yielded both the highest and lowest temperatures in the United States on the same day! Arizona is home to the Grand Canyon, known as one of the wonders of the world. Arizona has more national parks and monuments than any other state!

Arizona
48th state
February 14, 1912

Winslow, Arizona, is home to the world's best preserved **meteorite crater** on Earth. Approximately 50,000 years ago, an **ASTEROID** traveling **26,000 miles per hour** crashed into Earth. What remains is a large crater, nearly one mile across and **550 feet deep**.

GILA MONSTERS aren't monsters at all, but desert-dwelling lizards! They have **bead-like scales** and a thick tail which causes them to move slowly. Gila monsters don't have great eyesight. To find prey, they flick their **forked tongue** to smell their next meal.

STATE FACTS

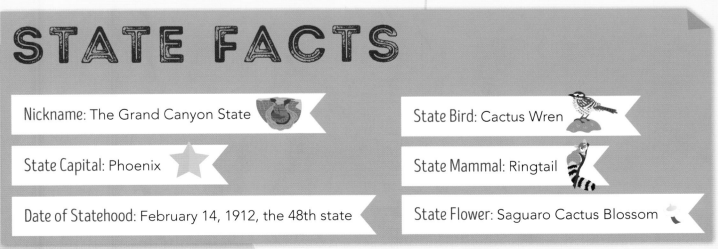

Nickname: The Grand Canyon State

State Capital: Phoenix

Date of Statehood: February 14, 1912, the 48th state

State Bird: Cactus Wren

State Mammal: Ringtail

State Flower: Saguaro Cactus Blossom

ARKANSAS

Use your stickers to fill in Arkansas's famous landmarks!

KANSAS

"The Spinach Capital of the World" is Alma, Arkansas. The town's water tower is even painted like a large can of **SPINACH**!

Atkins, Arkansas, holds **PICKLEFEST** every May, so it's not surprising that it is home to the first **fried dill pickle** ever sold.

HOT SPRINGS NATIONAL PARK was protected by Congress in 1832—40 years before Yellowstone became the first national park.

TEXAS

OKLAHOMA

Precious gems, such as **DIAMONDS**, can be found at **Crater of Diamonds State Park**.

STATE FACTS

Nickname: The Natural State

State Capital: Little Rock

Date of Statehood: June 15, 1836, 25th state

State Bird: Mockingbird

State Mammal: White-Tailed Deer

State Flower: Apple Blossom

MISSOURI

Arkansas, the 25th state, is located in the southeastern region of the United States. Three major Native American tribes, the Caddo, Osage, and Quapaw, lived in what is now present-day Arkansas. Arkansas is the home to over 600,000 acres of lakes and 9,700 miles of streams and rivers.

Arkansas
25th state
June 15, 1836

○ Alma

○ Atkins

LITTLE
ROCK

TENNESSEE

○ Hot Springs
National Park

MISSISSIPPI

○ Crater of Diamonds
State Park

MASTODON
fossils from the **Ice Age** were uncovered in eastern Arkansas.

LOUISIANA

CALIFORNIA

Use your stickers to fill in California's famous landmarks!

The tallest trees on Earth grow in northern California. The REDWOOD, or **Sequoia**, is a fast-growing tree that can grow more than **350 feet tall.** These giant trees can live to be **2,000 years old**!

SACRAMENTO

PACIFIC OCEAN

San Francisco

The GOLDEN GATE BRIDGE is a large, orange bridge built over the **Golden Gate Strait**, the entrance to the San Francisco Bay from the Pacific Ocean. It is an icon for the city of San Francisco.

California has **more than 1,000 miles of coastline** along the Pacific Ocean, and is home to some of the most beautiful BEACHES in America.

Los An

STATE FACTS

Nickname: The Golden State

State Capital: Sacramento

Date of Statehood: September 9, 1850, the 31st state

State Bird: California Valley Quail

State Mammal: Grizzly Bear

State Flower: Golden Poppy

Known as the "Golden State," California is the most populous state in America. It features a variety of landscapes. In some areas, you can travel to the beach, mountains, and desert all in one day! From the giant trees in the redwood forest, to the glamorous life of Hollywood, there's something for everyone in sunny California!

California
31st state
September 9, 1850

Yosemite Valley is home to cliffs, a variety of wildlife, and waterfalls. YOSEMITE FALLS is a **2,425-foot waterfall**, actually made up of **three smaller waterfalls**: upper Yosemite Fall, Middle Cascades, and lower Yosemite Fall.

Located in Los Angeles, California, the giant white letters of the HOLLYWOOD SIGN are a symbol for the movie and entertainment capital. Originally constructed for a housing development, the full sign once read "Hollywoodland." Each of the giant letters is **45 feet tall!**

HOLLYWOOD

COLORADO

Use your stickers to fill in Colorado's famous landmarks!

Vail, Colorado, is home to the third-largest ski resort in North America. Its **5,289 acres** are known for world-famous **SKIING**.

The song **"AMERICA, THE BEAUTIFUL,"** written by **Katharine Lee Bates**, was written after she visited **Pikes Peak** in 1893.

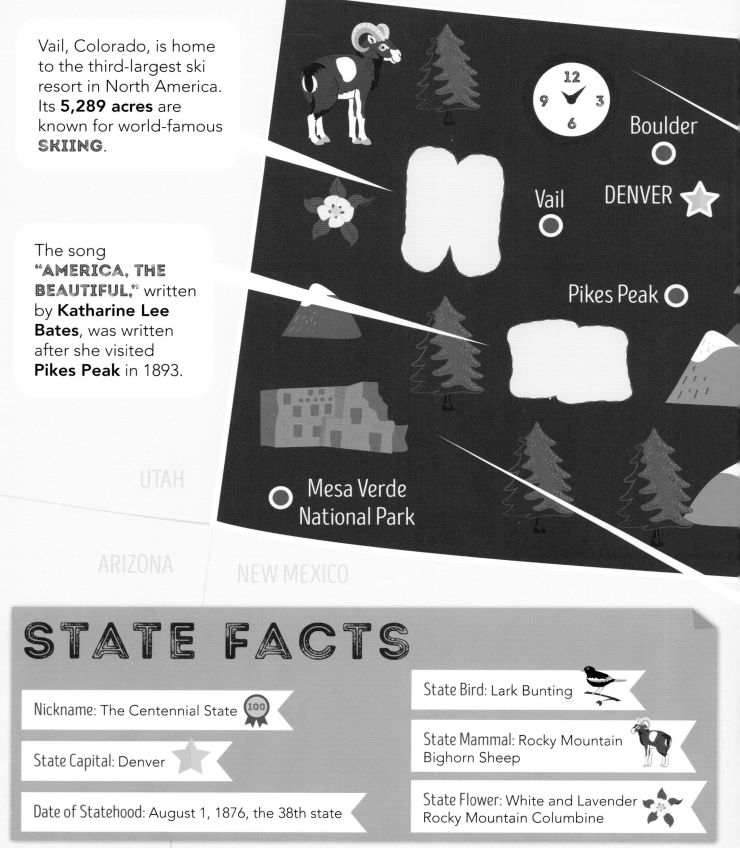

UTAH

ARIZONA

NEW MEXICO

Boulder

Vail

DENVER

Pikes Peak

Mesa Verde National Park

STATE FACTS

Nickname: The Centennial State

State Capital: Denver

Date of Statehood: August 1, 1876, the 38th state

State Bird: Lark Bunting

State Mammal: Rocky Mountain Bighorn Sheep

State Flower: White and Lavender Rocky Mountain Columbine

Colorado is part of the four corners, an area where four states (Utah, Colorado, Arizona, and New Mexico) meet. Colorado, meaning "colored red" in Spanish, has the highest elevation of all U.S. states. It is home to the Rocky Mountains, sweeping valleys, snow-covered peaks, and lush forests.

Colorado
38th state
August 1, 1876

The **NIST-F1 CESIUM FOUNTAIN ATOMIC CLOCK** in Boulder, Colorado, **keeps time for the entire country**. It will be accurate to the second for **80 million years**!

MESA VERDE NATIONAL PARK is home to **600 cliff dwellings** of the **Pueblo Native Americans**. The Pueblo lived there from 550 to 1300AD.

Every year, Colorado hosts the country's largest **RODEO**, called the Western Stock Show.

NEBRASKA

KANSAS

OKLAHOMA

TEXAS

CONNECTICUT

Use your stickers to fill in Connecticut's famous landmarks!

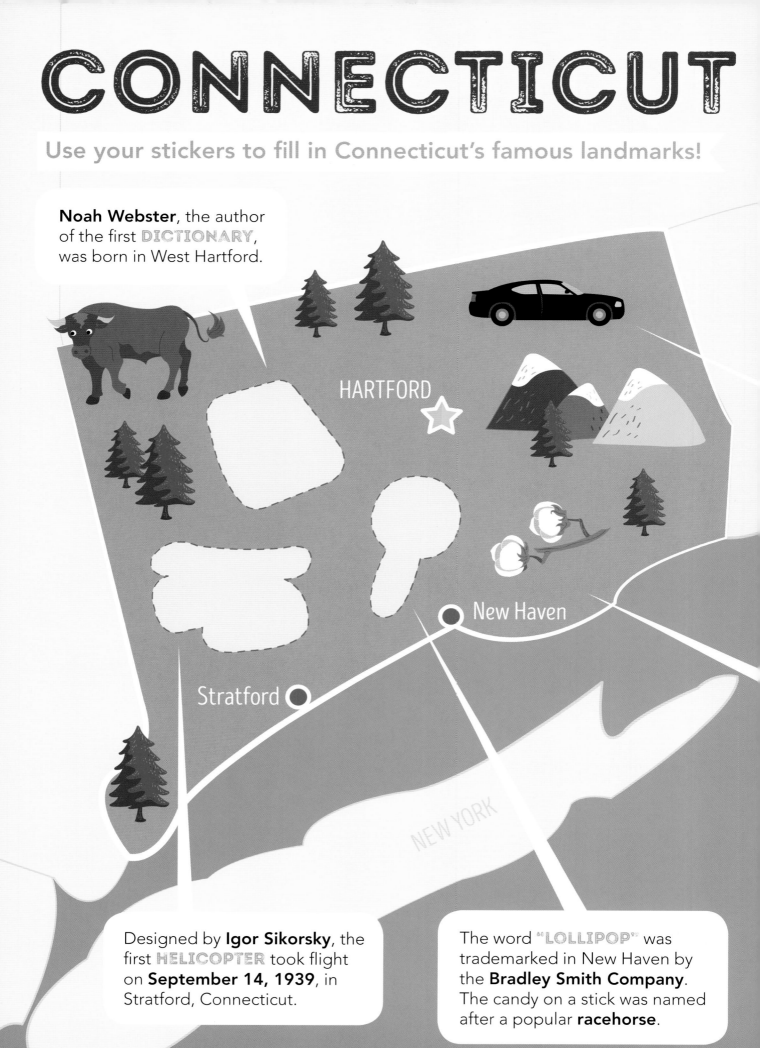

Noah Webster, the author of the first DICTIONARY, was born in West Hartford.

HARTFORD

New Haven

Stratford

NEW YORK

Designed by **Igor Sikorsky**, the first HELICOPTER took flight on **September 14, 1939**, in Stratford, Connecticut.

The word "LOLLIPOP" was trademarked in New Haven by the **Bradley Smith Company**. The candy on a stick was named after a popular **racehorse**.

One of the original thirteen colonies, Connecticut is located in the northeast of the United States. Nicknamed "the Constitution State," Connecticut played a vital role in the creation of the Constitution, the rules of our country. Connecticut's name derives from the Native American word meaning "land of the long tidal river." The state of Connecticut is home to flowing rivers, mountains, and forests.

Connecticut
5th state
January 9, 1788

In 1901, the FIRST AUTOMOTIVE LAW in the country was passed in Connecticut. The speed limit for automobiles was **12 miles per hour**.

The COTTON GIN, invented by **Eli Whitney in 1793**, was created in New Haven, Connecticut.

ATLANTIC OCEAN

STATE FACTS

Nickname: The Constitution State

State Capital: Hartford

Date of Statehood: January 9, 1788, the 5th state

State Bird: American Robin

State Marine Mammal: Sperm Whale

State Flower: Mountain Laurel

DELAWARE

Use your stickers to fill in Delaware's famous landmarks!

PENNSYLVANIA

● Wilmington

NEW JERSEY

Every summer, Wilmington, Delaware, hosts the **largest JAZZ FESTIVAL** on the **East Coast**.

BANK

DOVER

Delaware Bay

Delaware's official state insect is the **LADYBUG**. These spotted insects love to eat tiny bugs that feed on flowers, plants, and trees.

We the people

MARYLAND

Representatives from Delaware were the first to sign the **CONSTITUTION**, making Delaware the **first official state**.

Located along the Atlantic Ocean, Delaware has the lowest elevation of any state, and does not have any national parks. After Rhode Island, Delaware is the second smallest state. In 1638, Swedish settlers established the first European colony in present-day Delaware. It became the first state to ratify the Constitution in 1787.

Delaware
1st state
December 7, 1787

ATLANTIC OCEAN

Delaware Bay is home to the most HORSESHOE CRABS in the world.

Delaware is sometimes called the "DIAMOND STATE" because **President Thomas Jefferson** described Delaware as a **"jewel."**

STATE FACTS

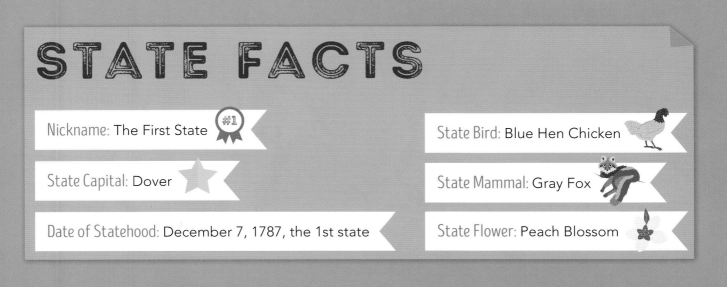

Nickname: The First State

State Capital: Dover

Date of Statehood: December 7, 1787, the 1st state

State Bird: Blue Hen Chicken

State Mammal: Gray Fox

State Flower: Peach Blossom

FLORIDA

Use your stickers to fill in Florida's famous landmarks!

ARKANSAS

Florida produces sixty percent of all the ORANGES grown in the United States.

Floridian **Benjamin Green**, a pharmacist and airman, developed the first SUNSCREEN in 1944.

ALABAMA

MISSISSIPPI

LOUISIANA

GULF OF MEXICO

Venice, Florida, is known as the SHARK TOOTH CAPITAL OF THE WORLD because of all the shark teeth that **wash up on its beaches**.

STATE FACTS

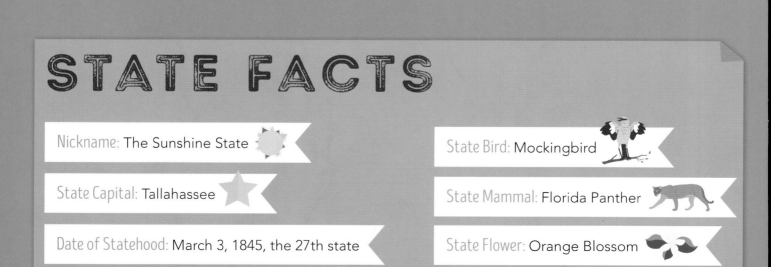

Nickname: The Sunshine State

State Capital: Tallahassee

Date of Statehood: March 3, 1845, the 27th state

State Bird: Mockingbird

State Mammal: Florida Panther

State Flower: Orange Blossom

Florida is located in the southeast of the United States. The modern-day state of Florida was discovered by explorer Juan Ponce de Leon in 1513. Saint Augustine, where Juan Ponce de Leon landed, is the oldest European settlement in Florida. It is the only state that borders both the Gulf of Mexico and the Atlantic Ocean. Florida, known as the Sunshine State, has warm weather, thousands of miles of coastlines, and a lot of orange groves!

Florida
27th state
March 3, 1845

GEORGIA

TALLAHASSEE

St. Augustine

The **launch pad** for many NASA SPACE FLIGHTS is located in Cape Canaveral, Florida.

Cape Canaveral

Venice

Florida is home to the BENWOOD SHIPWRECK in the **Florida Keys**. The Benwood sank in 1942 when it collided with another ship. The wreckage of the Benwood has become a **home to reef fish and other creatures**.

ATLANTIC OCEAN

GEORGIA

Use your stickers to fill in Georgia's famous landmarks!

TENNESSEE

ATLANTA

COCA-COLA was "born" in **1886** in Atlanta, Georgia, when pharmacist **John S. Pemberton** combined his specially created syrup with carbonated water.

SOUTH CAROLINA

More **PEANUTS** are grown in Georgia than in any other state in the country.

Vidalia

ALABAMA

FLORIDA

Famous **BASEBALL PLAYER Jackie Robinson** was born in Georgia in 1919.

GULF OF MEXICO

NORTH CAROLINA

Georgia, "the Peach State," is the largest state east of the Mississippi River. Georgia was named after British King George II, who created the colony in 1732. Georgia was the thirteenth state of the original thirteen colonies. Georgia is the largest producer in the United States of peaches, pecans, and peanuts.

Georgia
4th state
January 2, 1788

Famous for its **PEACHES**, Georgia uses **15,000 acres** —about the size of Manhattan—to grow them!

ATLANTIC OCEAN

The **VIDALIA ONION**, **a sweet onion,** can only be grown around Glennville and Vidalia, Georgia.

STATE FACTS

Nickname: The Peach State

State Capital: Atlanta

Date of Statehood: January 2, 1788, the 4th state

State Bird: Brown Thrasher

State Marine Mammal: Right Whale

State Flower: Cherokee Rose

HAWAII

On Kauai, island law states that no building should be taller than a **PALM TREE**.

Kauai

Oahu

HONOLULU

PACIFIC OCEAN

Oahu is the **most popular island for tourists**. Around one-third of Hawaii's best **SURFING** beaches are found on Oahu.

More than one-third of the world's **PINEAPPLES** are grown in Hawaii.

STATE FACTS

Nickname: The Aloha State

State Capital: Honolulu

Date of Statehood: August 21, 1959, the 50th state

State Bird: Nene

State Marine Mammal: Humpback Whale

State Flower: Yellow Hibiscus

The last state to join the United States of America, Hawaii is a group of volcanic islands located in the middle of the Pacific Ocean. Hawaii is known as the "Aloha State," which in Hawaiian means hello, welcome, love, and goodbye. Hawaii is a popular vacation destination and known for its lush forests, colorful coral reefs, and erupting volcanoes!

Hawaii
50th state
August 21, 1959

Maui

The eight main islands of Hawaii were all formed by underwater VOLCANOES. The warm tropical waters surrounding the islands are home to **many different types of sea life**.

Hawai'i

A LEI is a **special wreath made from flowers, seeds, or nuts**. It is presented as a gift to visitors as they arrive or depart.

IDAHO

Use your stickers to fill in Idaho's famous landmarks!

CANADA

WASHINGTON

The **DOG BARK PARK INN** in Cottonwood, Idaho, is the world's biggest beagle, and it's also a hotel!

OREGON

○ Cottonwood

Ernest Hemingway won the **Nobel Prize** for **LITERATURE** and lived in Sun Valley, Idaho, while writing *For Whom the Bell Tolls*.

○ Sun Valley

☆
BOISE

NEVADA

UTAH

Known as the "Niagara of the West," **SHOSHONE FALLS** is a **212-foot high** waterfall in Idaho.

Located in the northwest, Idaho was named by a miner who claimed it meant "gem of the mountains." Known for its potatoes, Idaho grows more potatoes than any other state. A scenic state, Idaho's rivers, mountains, and wildlife attract millions of visitors each year.

Idaho
43rd state
July 3, 1890

The first alpine **SKIING CHAIRLIFT** was built in Sun Valley, Idaho. In 1936, the fee to ride it was 25 cents!

Idaho is the leading producer of **POTATOES** in the United States. The state grows around **27 billion each year**!

MONTANA

WYOMING

NORTH DAKOTA

SOUTH DAKOTA

STATE FACTS

Nickname: The Gem State

State Capital: Boise

Date of Statehood: July 3, 1890, the 43rd state

State Bird: Mountain Bluebird

State Mammal: Appaloosa Horse

State Flower: Syringa

ILLINOIS

Use your stickers to fill in Illinois's famous landmarks!

IOWA

The **ICE CREAM SUNDAE** was invented in Evanston, Illinois.

Evanston

Chicago

Every **SAINT PATRICK'S DAY**, the Chicago River is **dyed green**.

SPRINGFIELD

Vandalia

MISSOURI

In **1893**, Chicago hosted the **World Exposition** and the **FERRIS WHEEL** was first introduced.

KENTUCKY

Located in the Midwest, Illinois has forests, prairies, and farmland. Chicago is one of the largest cities in the United States. The famous city is along the shores of Lake Michigan and is known for its architecture, museums, and Wrigley Field, the second-oldest ballpark in America.

Illinois
21st state
December 3, 1818

The **HOME INSURANCE BUILDING** was built in Chicago in **1885**. At the time, this **10-story-tall** building was known as the **world's first skyscraper**.

Vandalia, Illinois, is home to a **35-foot tall METAL DRAGON** that **breathes fire**.

STATE FACTS

Nickname: The Prairie State

State Capital: Springfield

Date of Statehood: December 3, 1818, the 21st state

State Bird: Cardinal

State Mammal: White-Tailed Deer

State Flower: Violet

INDIANA

Use your stickers to fill in Indiana's famous landmarks!

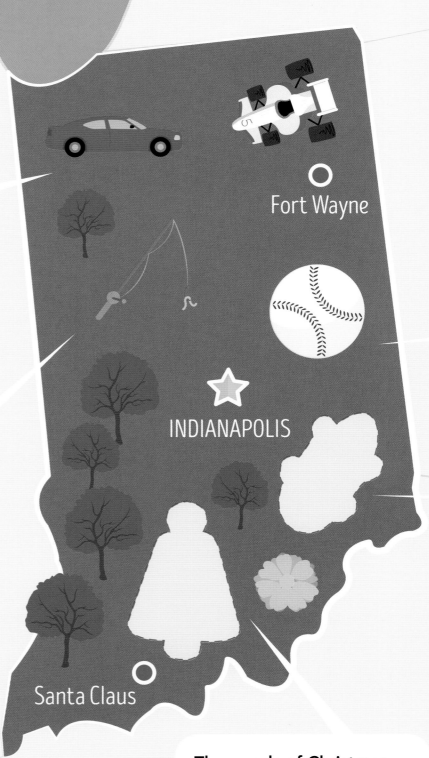

Indiana contains more HIGHWAYS per square mile than any other state.

In Indiana, it's **against the law** to CATCH FISH with dynamite or with your hands.

Thousands of Christmas lists are mailed to Santa Claus, Indiana, each year. Each letter receives a response signed by SANTA!

Indiana was named by Congress in 1800, and its name means "land of the Indians." The limestone found in Indiana has been used to build famous U.S. buildings such as the Empire State Building, Rockefeller Center, and the Pentagon. Indiana is also home to the Indianapolis 500—a famous automotive race.

Indiana
19th state
December 11, 1816

The first BASEBALL GAME took place in Fort Wayne in 1871.

WEST VIRGINIA

OHIO

Almost half of all cropland in Indiana is planted with CORN.

VIRGINIA

STATE FACTS

Nickname: The Hoosier State

State Bird: Cardinal

State Capital: Indianapolis

State Flower: Peony

Date of Statehood: December 11, 1816, the 19th state

IOWA

Use your stickers to fill in Iowa's famous landmarks!

SOUTH DAKOTA

MINNESOTA

A whopping **97 percent** of Iowa's land is used for FARMING.

Indianola, Iowa, is the home to the NATIONAL BALLOON MUSEUM, which celebrates over **200 years** of ballooning. The museum displays **hot-air balloons** in all sorts of sizes, colors, and shapes.

Cedar Rapids

DES MOINES

Indianola

NEBRASKA

STATE FACTS

Nickname: The Hawkeye State

State Capital: Des Moines

Date of Statehood: December 28, 1846, the 29th state

State Bird: Eastern Goldfinch

State Flower: Wild Rose

KANSAS

Iowa, nicknamed the Hawkeye State, is the only state in the country that is sandwiched between rivers. The Mississippi River flows along Iowa's entire eastern border, and the Missouri River, along with its tributary the Big Sioux, form the entire western border. Iowa is also home to the first corn palace and "crookedest" street in the world.

Iowa
29th state
December 28, 1846

Strawberry Point

Le Claire

MICHIGAN

The **world's largest STRAWBERRY** can be found in Strawberry Point, Iowa.

INDIANA

Buffalo Bill, also known as **William Cody**, PONY EXPRESS RIDER and showman, was born in Le Claire, Iowa.

ILLINOIS

The largest CEREAL MILL in the United States is in Cedar Rapids.

MISSOURI

KANSAS

Use your stickers to fill in Kansas's famous landmarks!

NEBRASKA

Cawker City, Kansas, is home to a **BALL OF TWINE** that **weighs more than three rhinoceroses**!

COLORADO

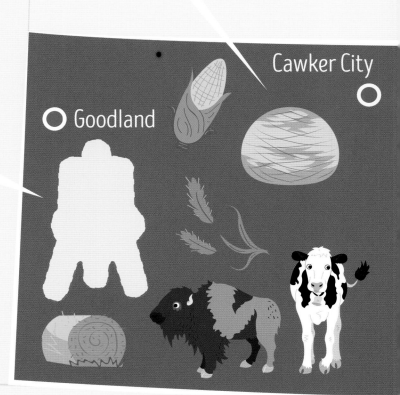

Cawker City

Goodland

Goodland, Kansas, is home to the **WORLD'S LARGEST EASEL** at **80 feet tall**! A replica of **Vincent Van Gogh's *Sunflowers*** is displayed on the easel.

NEW MEXICO

STATE FACTS

Nickname: The Sunflower State

State Capital: Topeka

Date of Statehood: January 29, 1861, the 34th state

State Bird: Western Meadowlark

State Mammal: American Buffalo

State Flower: Wild Native Sunflower

TEXAS

Located in the heart of the Midwest, Kansas has vast plains and rolling wheat fields. Kansas is right in the middle of "Tornado Alley." In the late spring and early fall, giant storms form over Kansas's plains, often turning into fast and powerful tornadoes. Kansas was also the home of Dorothy Gale in L. Frank Baum's famous book *The Wizard of Oz*.

Kansas
34th state
January 29, 1861

Atchison

TOPEKA

Hutchinson

Wichita

Pioneering pilot AMELIA EARHART, born in Atchison, Kansas, was the **first woman to fly across the Pacific and Atlantic Oceans.** She vanished as she was attempting the first around-the-world flight by a female pilot.

The Kansas UNDERGROUND SALT MUSEUM is also a working mine, and is **65 stories** below Hutchinson, Kansas.

Underwater archaeologist ROBERT BALLARD was born in land-locked Wichita, Kansas. He discovered the sunken *Titanic* and other notable ships.

MISSOURI

OKLAHOMA

ILLINOIS

ARKANSAS

37

KENTUCKY

Use your stickers to fill in Kentucky's famous landmarks!

Held in Louisville, the **KENTUCKY DERBY** is an **annual horse race** that draws over **150,000 visitors** each year.

Thomas Edison introduced his invention of the **LIGHT BULB** at the **Southern Exposition** in Louisville, Kentucky, in **1883**.

ILLINOIS

OHIO

INDIANA

FRANKFORT

Louisville

TENNESSEE

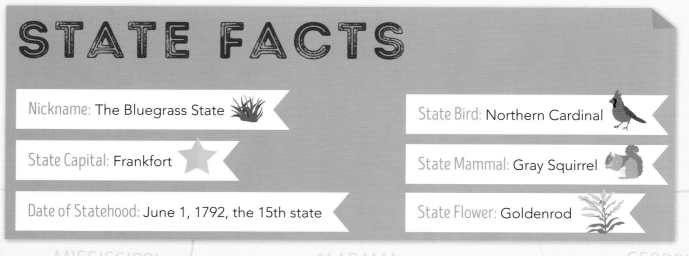

STATE FACTS

Nickname: The Bluegrass State

State Capital: Frankfort

Date of Statehood: June 1, 1792, the 15th state

State Bird: Northern Cardinal

State Mammal: Gray Squirrel

State Flower: Goldenrod

MISSISSIPPI   ALABAMA   GEORGIA

Known as the "Bluegrass State," Kentucky is the birthplace of bluegrass music, a type of folk music. The state of Kentucky is full of running water—in fact, the only other state with more running water is Alaska. President Abraham Lincoln was famously born in a one-room log cabin in the woods of Kentucky.

Kentucky
15th state
June 1, 1792

PENNSYLVANIA

WEST VIRGINIA

VIRGINIA

NORTH CAROLINA

SOUTH CAROLINA

Kentucky is the home state of America's sixteenth president, ABRAHAM LINCOLN.

In 1893, the song "HAPPY BIRTHDAY TO YOU" was written in Louisville by two sisters.

Cassius Marcellus Clay Jr., also known as MUHAMMAD ALI, three-time world heavyweight boxing champion, was born in Louisville, Kentucky.

LOUISIANA

Use your stickers to fill in Louisiana's famous landmarks!

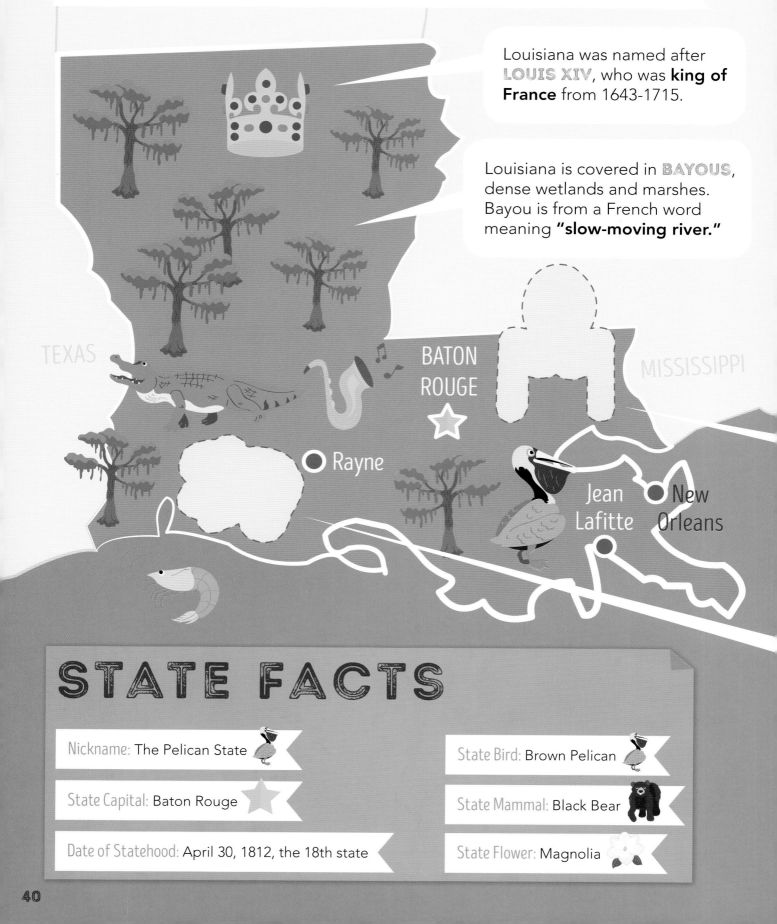

Louisiana was named after **LOUIS XIV**, who was **king of France** from 1643-1715.

Louisiana is covered in **BAYOUS**, dense wetlands and marshes. Bayou is from a French word meaning **"slow-moving river."**

ARKANSAS

TEXAS

BATON ROUGE

MISSISSIPPI

Rayne

Jean Lafitte

New Orleans

STATE FACTS

Nickname: The Pelican State

State Capital: Baton Rouge

Date of Statehood: April 30, 1812, the 18th state

State Bird: Brown Pelican

State Mammal: Black Bear

State Flower: Magnolia

In 1803, the territory of the United States doubled in size with President Thomas Jefferson's Louisiana Purchase. The modern-day state of Louisiana became the first state created out of the Louisiana Purchase. It is located on the Gulf of Mexico. In 2005, Hurricane Katrina, one of the strongest hurricanes in U.S. history, demolished parts of Louisiana.

Louisiana
18th state
April 30, 1812

FLORIDA

MARDI GRAS is a celebration of food and fun in **New Orleans**. The official colors for the holiday are **green, gold, and purple**.

The town of Jean Lafitte, Louisiana, is named after the notorious French PIRATE **Jean Lafitte**, who led a band of pirates that sailed the **Gulf of Mexico**.

Rayne, Louisiana, is known as the FROG **capital of the world**.

GULF OF
MEXICO

MAINE

Use your stickers to fill in Maine's famous landmarks!

Maine produces **99 percent** of the **BLUEBERRIES** in the country.

CANADA

Hanson Gregory from Camden, Maine, claims to have invented the **DOUGHNUT** while at sea.

West Quoddy Head

Because they **live farther east** than anyone else in America, the residents of West Quoddy Head, Maine, are the first people to see the **SUNRISE** each morning.

Maine is the furthest northeastern state in the United States. Maine has rocky coastlines dotted with lighthouses and scenic lakes, streams, and mountains. Maine is known for producing lots of blueberries and lobsters!

Maine
23rd state
March 15, 1820

AUGUSTA

Camden

ATLANTIC OCEAN

STATE FACTS

Nickname: The Pine Tree State

State Capital: Augusta

Date of Statehood: March 15, 1820, the 23rd state

State Bird: Chickadee

State Mammal: Moose

State Flower: White Pine Cone and Tassel

MARYLAND

Use your stickers to fill in Maryland's famous landmarks!

One of the original thirteen colonies, **Maryland** originally gave up some of its land to form Washington, D.C. It has thousands of miles of coastline on the Atlantic Ocean and Chesapeake Bay. Often called "America in Miniature," Maryland has everything from forests to beaches.

Maryland
7th state
April 28, 1788

Edgar Allen Poe, a nineteenth-century American **writer** who wrote **"THE RAVEN,"** lived and died in Baltimore.

WILD PONIES live on an **island** off the coast of Maryland.

Annapolis, Maryland, is known as the **SAILING** capital of the world.

PENNSYLVANIA

NEW YORK

Baltimore
ANNAPOLIS

ATLANTIC OCEAN

DELAWARE

Chesapeake Bay

America's national anthem, **"THE STAR-SPANGLED BANNER,"** was written by **Francis Scott Key** in Maryland's Chesapeake Bay during the **War of 1812**.

VIRGINIA

STATE FACTS

Nickname: The Old Line State

State Capital: Annapolis

Date of Statehood: April 28, 1788, the 7th state

State Bird: Baltimore Oriole

State Flower: Black-Eyed Susan

MASSACHUSETTS

Use your stickers to fill in Massachusetts's famous landmarks!

VERMONT

The first **LIGHTHOUSE** in the United States was built in **1716** in **Boston Harbor**.

Alexander Graham Bell made the first **TELEPHONE** call ever from his Boston, Massachusetts, laboratory in **1876**.

NEW HAMPSHIRE

NEW YORK

The first **BASKETBALL GAME** was played in **Springfield, Massachusetts, in 1891**. Originally, a **soccer ball** was used with a **peach basket**.

Springfield

CONNECTICUT

STATE FACTS

Nickname: The Bay State

State Capital: Boston

Date of Statehood: February 6, 1788, the 6th state

State Bird: Black-Capped Chickadee

State Marine Mammal: Right Whale

State Flower: Mayflower

One of the original thirteen colonies, **Massachusetts** is located in the New England region of the United States. It is famously known for the landing of the Mayflower and Pilgrims at Plymouth Rock in 1620. During the American Revolution, Boston Harbor was the setting for the Boston Tea Party, an event in which hundreds of crates of tea were dumped overboard to protest unfair taxes.

Massachusetts
6th state
February 6, 1788

MAINE

BOSTON

Plymouth

RHODE ISLAND

ATLANTIC OCEAN

Every year, thousands of visitors go to Massachusetts to **whale watch**. The migration route of humpback, minke, and fin WHALES passes right by the Massachusetts coast.

Seeking religious freedom, the **Pilgrims** boarded the MAYFLOWER in England, crossed the **Atlantic Ocean,** and landed on **Plymouth, Massachusetts,** in 1620.

MICHIGAN

Use your stickers to fill in Michigan's famous landmarks!

Michigan grows up to **75 percent** of the tart CHERRIES in the United States.

Michigan State University has a collection of **156 mammal** BRAINS.

Colon, Michigan, "magic capital of the world" is home to the **largest manufacturer** of MAGIC SUPPLIES.

MINNESOTA

WISCONSIN

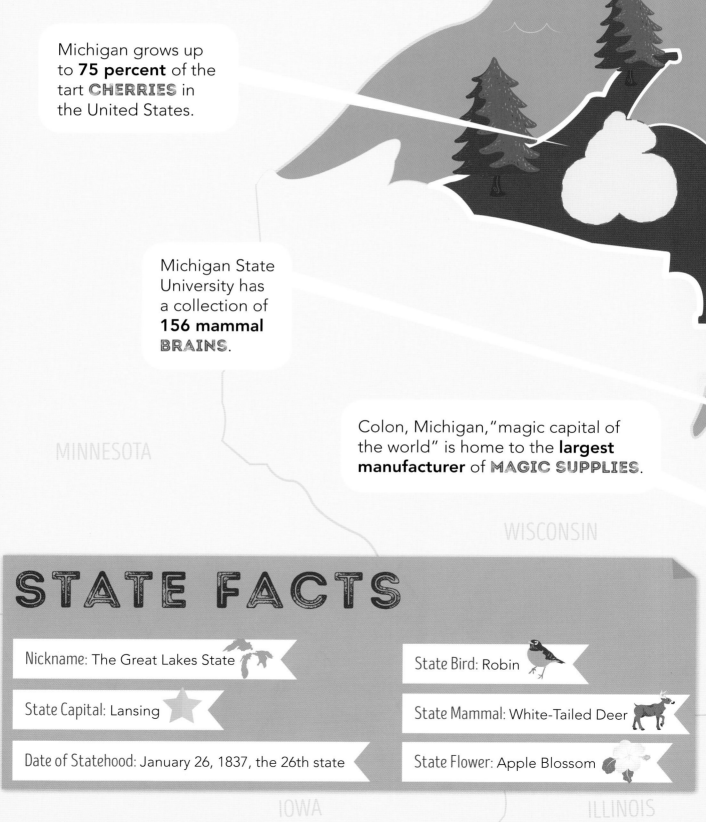

STATE FACTS

Nickname: The Great Lakes State

State Capital: Lansing

Date of Statehood: January 26, 1837, the 26th state

State Bird: Robin

State Mammal: White-Tailed Deer

State Flower: Apple Blossom

IOWA

ILLINOIS

Located on the Great Lakes, Michigan is home to the country's longest freshwater shoreline. Detroit, Michigan, is known as the "car capital of the world." In fact, Henry Ford, born in Greenfield Township, invented the assembly line for mass production and the Model T automobile.

Michigan
26th state
January 26, 1837

LAKE SUPERIOR

LAKE MICHIGAN

LAKE HURON

Detroit, Michigan, the state's largest city, is known as "MOTOR CITY" because of all of the **cars** made there.

CANADA

LANSING

Michigan State University

Detroit

LAKE ERIE

Colon

INDIANA

OHIO

MINNESOTA

Use your stickers to fill in Minnesota's famous landmarks!

Water skis and SNOWMOBILES were invented in Minnesota.

NORTH DAKOTA

The **land of 10,000 LAKES** has over **90,000 miles of shoreline**. That's more shoreline than California, Florida, and Hawaii combined!

SOUTH DAKOTA

Minnesota is home to three million COWS.

ST. PAUL ☆
Mall of America ⭕

IOWA

Located along the Canadian border, Minnesota is home to many lakes—over 10,000 of them—popular for water skiing in the summer and snowmobiling in the winter. Along with a wide variety of wildlife, Minnesota is also the starting point for the Mississippi River.

Minnesota
32nd state
May 11, 1858

CANADA

LAKE SUPERIOR

MICHIGAN

LAKE MICHIGAN

WISCONSIN

Minnesota is home to the largest population of TIMBER WOLVES in the continental U.S.

A popular tourist site in Minnesota, the MALL OF AMERICA is so big 78 football fields could fit inside!

STATE FACTS

Nickname: Land of 10,000 Lakes

State Capital: St. Paul

Date of Statehood: May 11, 1858, the 32nd state

State Bird: Common Loon

State Flower: Pink and White Lady's Slipper

MISSISSIPPI

Use your stickers to fill in Mississippi's famous landmarks!

ARKANSAS

ALABAMA

The Mississippi River is famous for the **RIVERBOATS** that tour up and down its shores.

Mississippi River

The only **CACTUS PLANTATION** **in the world** can be found in Edwards, Mississippi.

Edwards

JACKSON

Vicksburg

LOUISIANA

SHOES weren't always sold in pairs! **Phil Gilbert's shoe parlor** in Vicksburg, Mississippi, was the first to sell shoes in pairs.

Biloxi

GULF OF MEXICO

Mississippi, a southern state, is covered in forests, and has more tree farms than any other state. The name Mississippi comes from a Native American word meaning "Father of Waters." In addition to the Mississippi River, the state is also located along the Gulf of Mexico. Mississippi is known for its historic plantations and its main crop, cotton.

Mississippi
20th state
December 10, 1817

The creation of the TEDDY BEAR was inspired by a bear that President **Theodore Roosevelt** saw on a trip in Mississippi.

Invented in Biloxi in **1898**, ROOT BEER was created by **Edward Adolf Barq, Sr.**

STATE FACTS

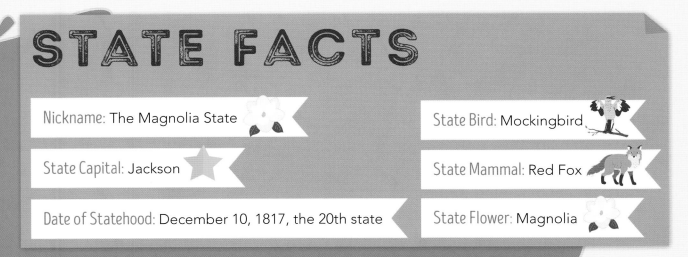

Nickname: The Magnolia State

State Capital: Jackson

Date of Statehood: December 10, 1817, the 20th state

State Bird: Mockingbird

State Mammal: Red Fox

State Flower: Magnolia

MISSOURI

Use your stickers to fill in Missouri's famous landmarks!

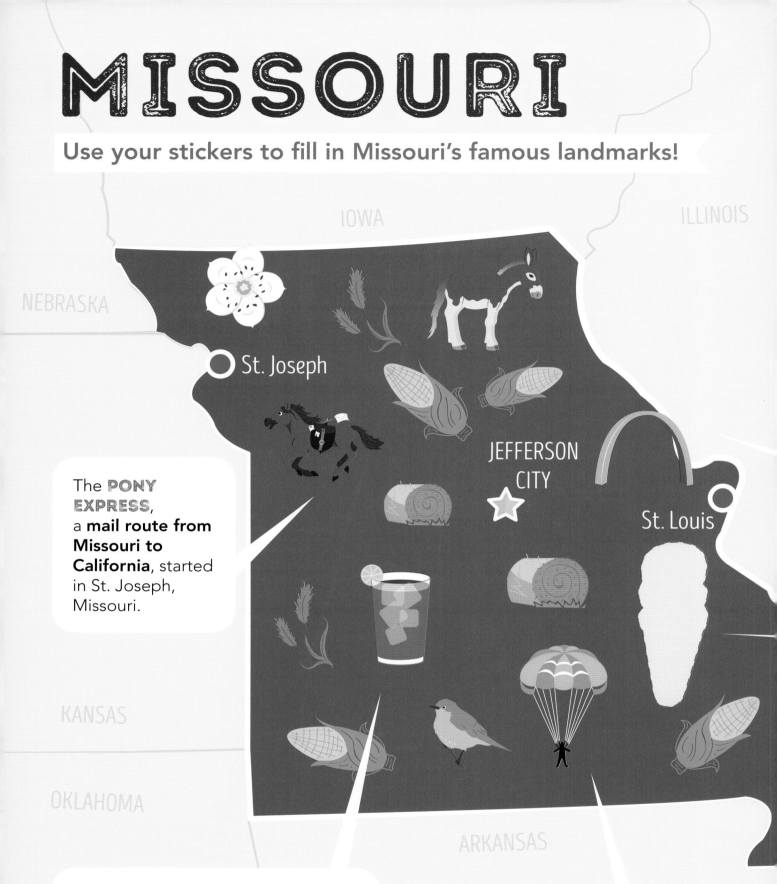

NEBRASKA

IOWA

ILLINOIS

St. Joseph

JEFFERSON CITY

St. Louis

KANSAS

OKLAHOMA

ARKANSAS

The **PONY EXPRESS**, a **mail route from Missouri to California**, started in St. Joseph, Missouri.

The ice cream cone wasn't the only cold invention at the **1904 World's Fair** in St. Louis. **Richard Blechyden** created the first **ICED TEA** there too.

In **1912** near St. Louis, Captain **Albert Berry** was the first person to successfully **PARACHUTE** out of an airplane.

Missouri is located in the heart of the Midwest and is known for its cropland, the Pony Express, and the St. Louis World's Fair in 1904. Famous Missourians include American author Mark Twain and outlaw Jesse James.

Missouri
24th state
August 10, 1821

The **ST. LOUIS ARCH**, or **Gateway Arch**, symbolizes the westward expansion of the United States. It is the world's tallest arch at **630 feet high**.

St. Louis, Missouri, is the birthplace of the **ICE-CREAM CONE**. At the **World's Fair in 1904**, an ice-cream vendor ran out of paper cups and instead rolled up a **waffle** to hold the ice cream!

STATE FACTS

Nickname: The Show-Me State

State Capital: Jefferson City

Date of Statehood: August 10, 1821, the 24th state

State Bird: Bluebird

State Mammal: Missouri Mule

State Flower: White Hawthorn Blossom

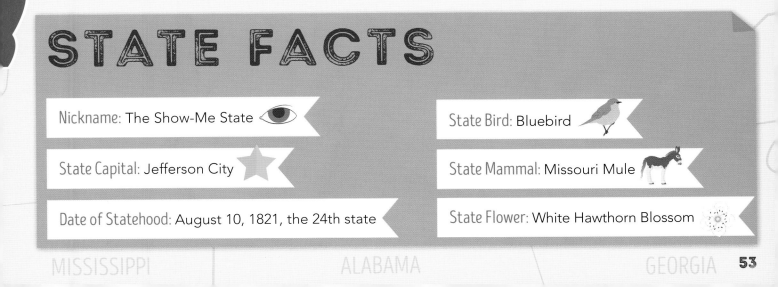

MONTANA

Use your stickers to fill in Montana's famous landmarks!

CANADA

IDAHO

Shelby

HELENA

Miles City

WYOMING

Jack Horner, born in Shelby, Montana, discovered many DINOSAUR species and inspired *Jurassic Park's* **Dr. Alan Grant**.

Montana is known as the TREASURE STATE because of all the **gold, silver, and copper** buried under its mountains.

Miles City, Montana, is known as the COWBOY **capital of the world**.

STATE FACTS

Nickname: The Treasure State

State Capital: Helena

Date of Statehood: November 8, 1889, the 41st state

State Bird: Western Meadowlark

State Mammal: Grizzly Bear

State Flower: Bitterroot

UTAH

COLORADO

NEBRASKA

Use your stickers to fill in Nebraska's famous landmarks!

The **LIED JUNGLE** in **Henry Doorly's Zoo** in Omaha, Nebraska, is the **biggest indoor rainforest** in the United States.

NORTH DAKOTA

SOUTH DAKOTA

IOWA

COLORADO

Omaha

LINCOLN

KANSAS

Nebraska is **95 percent farmland**. **CORN** is one of Nebraska's most important crops.

One of the **world's biggest WOOLLY MAMMOTH** fossils was found in Lincoln, Nebraska.

STATE FACTS

Nickname: The Cornhusker State

State Bird: Western Meadowlark

State Capital: Lincoln

State Mammal: White-Tailed Deer

Date of Statehood: March 1, 1867, the 37th state

State Flower: Goldenrod

NEVADA

Use your stickers to fill in Nevada's famous landmarks!

Nevada produces the **most GOLD in the nation**. In the entire world, only South Africa produces more.

CARSON CITY

CALIFORNIA

CAMELS were used as pack animals in Nevada in the late 1800s.

There is enough concrete in the **HOOVER DAM** on the **Nevada-Arizona border** to build a four-foot-wide sidewalk around the Earth's equator.

ARIZONA

Nevada is mostly desert, but is also home to more mountain ranges than any other state. Nevada has a rich history of mining. In 1859, a rich silver deposit was discovered in Nevada. Gold, zinc, copper, mercury, and lead have also been found in Nevada.

Nevada
36th state
October 31, 1864

KANGAROO RATS in Nevada's deserts can live their whole life **without drinking one drop of water**.

Nearly all of Nevada is located in the **Great Basin Desert**, and is known as a "COLD" DESERT because most of its precipitation comes in the form of **snow**.

UTAH

COLORADO

STATE FACTS

Nickname: The Silver State

State Capital: Carson City

Date of Statehood: October 31, 1864, the 36th state

State Bird: Mountain Bluebird

State Mammal: Desert Bighorn Sheep

State Flower: Sagebrush

NEW MEXICO

NEW HAMPSHIRE

Use your stickers to fill in New Hampshire's famous landmarks!

CANADA

New Hampshire's **MOUNT WASHINGTON** is the highest peak in the northeastern United States and is known for its **wild weather**. To get to the summit, visitors can drive the mountain road, take a cog railway, or hike the steep slopes.

The first **ALARM CLOCK** was invented in Concord, New Hampshire.

○ Mount Washington

VERMONT

Peterborough, New Hampshire, opened the first **PUBLIC LIBRARY** in the United States.

12
9   3
6

CONCORD

Derry

○ Peterborough

NEW YORK

MASSACHUSETTS

MAINE

Located in the northeast and bordering Canada, New Hampshire is known for its lakes, scenic landscapes, and stunning mountains. Covered in maple trees, New Hampshire is one of the top producers of maple syrup in the nation.

New Hampshire
9th state
June 21, 1788

Alan Shepard, born in Derry, New Hampshire, was the **first American** to TRAVEL INTO SPACE.

ATLANTIC OCEAN

STATE FACTS

Nickname: The Granite State

State Capital: Concord

Date of Statehood: June 21, 1788, the 9th state

State Bird: Purple Finch

State Mammal: White-Tailed Deer

State Flower: Purple Lilac

NEW JERSEY

Use your stickers to fill in New Jersey's famous landmarks!

NEW YORK

The **first BASEBALL GAME** was played in Hoboken, New Jersey.

Hoboken

PENNSYLVANIA

TRENTON

The first full **complete skeleton** of a **DINOSAUR** was discovered in **1858** in Haddonfield, New Jersey.

Camden

Haddonfield

SALT WATER TAFFY was created in the **1880s** on the **Atlantic City boardwalk**.

Atlantic City

MARYLAND

DELAWARE

One of the original thirteen colonies, New Jersey is known as the "Garden State." It is located between Pennsylvania and New York and is named after England's city, Jersey. It is the most densely populated state in the U.S.

New Jersey
3rd state
December 18, 1787

New Jersey has the most DINERS in the United States.

ATLANTIC OCEAN

In 1933, the first DRIVE-IN MOVIE THEATER opened in Camden, New Jersey.

STATE FACTS

Nickname: The Garden State

State Capital: Trenton

Date of Statehood: December 18, 1787, the 3rd state

State Bird: Eastern Goldfinch

State Mammal: Horse

State Flower: Violet

NEW MEXICO

Use your stickers to fill in New Mexico's famous landmarks!

UTAH | COLORADO

ARIZONA

One of the **most famous female** ARTISTS of the twentieth century, **Georgia O'Keefe,** lived in Santa Fe, New Mexico.

SANTA FE

Albuquerque

Roswell

MEXICO

ADOBE **(a mix of sand, straw, soil, and water)** is used to **build many homes** in New Mexico.

New Mexico consists of vast deserts, mountainous regions, forests, and caverns. For nearly twenty thousand years, the Pueblo, Apache, Comanche, Navajo, and Ute Native Americans lived in present-day New Mexico. New Mexico's history is visible through the Spanish missions and Native American buildings and structures that are still standing today!

New Mexico
47th state
January 6, 1912

The **AMERICAN INTERNATIONAL RATTLESNAKE MUSEUM** in Albuquerque, New Mexico, has the **world's biggest collection of live rattlesnakes**.

OKLAHOMA

The world's largest **HOT-AIR BALLOON FESTIVAL** takes place in Albuquerque every October.

Roswell, New Mexico, is the home of the **INTERNATIONAL UFO MUSEUM**, which was opened after a **mysterious object** crashed near Roswell in **1947**.

TEXAS

STATE FACTS

Nickname: Land of Enchantment

State Capital: Santa Fe

Date of Statehood: January 6, 1912, the 47th state

State Bird: Greater Roadrunner

State Mammal: American Black Bear

State Flower: Yucca

NEW YORK

Use your stickers to fill in New York's famous landmarks!

CANADA

LAKE HURON

NORMAN ROCKWELL, painter and illustrator, was born in Manhattan, New York.

BROADWAY is the **theater district** of New York City, famous for its **plays and musicals**.

LAKE ONTARIO

Coney Island, located near New York City, is a popular **amusement park** and was also the birthplace of the **HOT DOG**!

LAKE ERIE

PENNSYLVANIA

STATE FACTS

Nickname: The Empire State

State Capital: Albany

Date of Statehood: July 26, 1788, the 11th state

State Bird: Bluebird

State Mammal: Beaver

State Flower: Rose

OHIO

Whether it's New York City, Niagara Falls, or the Erie Canal, New York is home to many famous American landmarks. One of the original thirteen colonies, New York is home to Ellis Island which became an immigration hub as immigrants from Europe entered the country in the late nineteenth and twentieth centuries.

New York
11th state
July 26, 1788

MAINE

VERMONT

ALBANY

MASSACHUSETTS

ATLANTIC OCEAN

CONNECTICUT

RHODE ISLAND

Manhattan

New York City

Coney Island

NEW JERSEY

Located in **New York Harbor**, the STATUE OF LIBERTY was a birthday gift from France, celebrating America's **one-hundredth birthday**.

In **1983**, the CONEY ISLAND MERMAID PARADE was founded. Each year, thousands of people in **mermaid costumes** gather on floats to celebrate the **beginning of summer**.

NORTH CAROLINA

Use your stickers to fill in North Carolina's famous landmarks!

Dolley Madison, born in Guilford County, North Carolina, was married to **President James Madison**. She started the tradition of the annual EASTER EGG ROLL on the **White House lawn**.

On **December 17, 1903**, the WRIGHT BROTHERS completed the **first successful flight** of a mechanically propelled airplane at Kitty Hawk, North Carolina.

OHIO

WEST VIRGINIA

KENTUCKY

VIRGINIA

TENNESSEE

RALEIGH

Guilford County

GEORGIA

SOUTH CAROLINA

STATE FACTS

Nickname: The Tar Heel State

State Capital: Raleigh

Date of Statehood: November 21, 1789, the 12th state

State Bird: Cardinal

State Mammal: Gray Squirrel

State Flower: Dogwood

One of the original thirteen colonies, North Carolina is situated along the Atlantic coast. It features sprawling, white sandy beaches and land for agriculture. In fact, North Carolina grows the most sweet potatoes in the United States. North Carolina is famously known as the site of the first airplane flight of the Wright Brothers.

North Carolina
12th state
November 21, 1789

Kitty Hawk
Roanoke Island

In **1587**, the FIRST NON-NATIVE BABY BORN IN AMERICA was born on Roanoke Island.

Hampstead

The VENUS FLYTRAP, a **plant that "eats" insects**, is native to Hampstead, North Carolina.

ATLANTIC OCEAN

Use your stickers to fill in North Dakota's famous landmarks!

CANADA

Dakota Dinosaur Museum

BISMARCK

SOUTH DAKOTA

A complete **TRICERATOPS** fossil is on display at the **Dakota Dinosaur Museum**.

North Dakota produces more **HONEY** than any other state.

In **1887**, **David Henderson Houston** invented a **CAMERA** in North Dakota. He scrambled the letters in "Dakota" and called it **Kodak**.

Although it's the least visited state, North Dakota is located in the geographic center of North America. It's located above South Dakota and below Canada. North Dakota's land is covered in crops, with farmland taking up 90 percent of the state.

North Dakota
39th state
November 2, 1889

More **SUNFLOWERS** are grown in North Dakota than in any other state.

While journeying to the **Pacific in 1804-06, explorers Lewis and Clark** encountered their first **GRIZZLY BEARS** in North Dakota.

MINNESOTA

STATE FACTS

Nickname: The Peace Garden State

State Capital: Bismarck

Date of Statehood: November 2, 1889, the 39th state

State Bird: Western Meadowlark

State Flower: Wild Prairie Rose

OHIO

MICHIGAN

CANADA

Use your stickers to fill in Ohio's famous landmarks!

Ohio's **GOODYEAR BLIMP** only weighs **between 100 and 200 pounds** when it's inflated with helium.

LAKE ERIE

INDIANA

COLUMBUS

Neil Armstrong, the first man to walk on the Moon, is from Ohio. More **ASTRONAUTS** are from Ohio than any other state.

WEST VIRGINIA

On **February 20, 1962, John Glenn**, an Ohio native, was the first American to **ORBIT EARTH**.

STATE FACTS

Nickname: The Buckeye State

State Capital: Columbus

Date of Statehood: March 1, 1803, the 17th state

State Bird: Cardinal

State Mammal: White-Tailed Deer

State Flower: Scarlet Carnation

KENTUCKY

OKLAHOMA

Use your stickers to fill in Oklahoma's famous landmarks!

Okmulgee, Oklahoma, holds the record for the **biggest** PECAN PIE.

KANSAS

TEXAS

All AIRPLANES in the United States are registered in Oklahoma.

Okmulgee

OKLAHOMA CITY

Known as the "Oklahoma Land Rush," in 1889 the land was opened up to settlers and 50,000 people swarmed the area to settle there. The Dust Bowl, a severe drought and high winds during the 1930s, destroyed much of Oklahoma. As a result, more than a million Oklahoma residents left for California.

Oklahoma
46th state
November 16, 1907

More TORNADOES occur in Oklahoma than in any other state. A tornado's whirling winds can reach speeds of up **to 300 miles per hour**.

STATE FACTS

Nickname: The Sooner State

State Capital: Oklahoma City

Date of Statehood: November 16, 1907, the 46th state

State Bird: Scissor-Tailed Flycatcher

State Mammal: American Buffalo

State Flower: Oklahoma Rose

MEXICO

OREGON

Use your stickers to fill in Oregon's famous landmarks!

WASHINGTON

Nine **LIGHTHOUSES** line the Oregon coast.

SALEM

Carousel Museum

PACIFIC OCEAN

Crater Lake

Crater Lake, the **deepest lake in the United States**, was formed 7,700 years ago by the **eruption** of the **VOLCANO** Mount Mazama.

Oregon's **CAROUSEL MUSEUM** contains the **world's largest collection of carousel horses**.

CALIFORNIA

NEVADA

Located in the western region of the United States, Oregon is situated along the Pacific Ocean. It has a diverse landscape, ranging from beaches, mountains, and valleys. Oregon is of course known for the Oregon Trail, an emigration path from Missouri to Oregon.

Oregon
33rd state
February 14, 1859

IDAHO

Oregon is the only state in America that has an **official state nut**—the HAZELNUT.

MONTANA

The OREGON TRAIL played an important role in America's westward expansion. People traveled in **covered wagons** along the trail.

WYOMING

STATE FACTS

Nickname: The Beaver State

State Bird: Western Meadowlark

State Capital: Salem

State Mammal: Beaver

Date of Statehood: February 14, 1859, the 33rd state

State Flower: Oregon Grape

UTAH

PENNSYLVANIA

Use your stickers to fill in Pennsylvania's famous landmarks!

CANADA

NEW YORK

LAKE ERIE

Hershey, Pennsylvania, is known as the **CHOCOLATE** capital of the world.

OHIO

Gobbler's Knob

Hershey

HARRISBURG

WEST VIRGINIA

MARYLAND

Every **February 2nd**, people gather in Gobbler's Knob, Pennsylvania, to watch **PUNXSUTAWNEY PHIL** the **groundhog**. It's said that if he comes out of his burrow and sees his **shadow**, there will be six more weeks of wintery weather. If he doesn't see his shadow, there will be an early start to spring.

Pennsylvania's **state insect** is the **FIREFLY**.

VIRGINIA

Founded by William Penn, Pennsylvania was established as a home for the Quakers. Pennsylvania has played a vital role in American history including the creation of the Declaration of Independence, being the second state to ratify the Constitution, and as the site of the Battle of Gettysburg during the Civil War.

Pennsylvania
2nd state
December 12, 1787

DAILY NEWS

America's first **DAILY NEWSPAPER** was published in Philadelphia in **1784**.

NEW JERSEY

ATLANTIC OCEAN

● Philadelphia

The **LIBERTY BELL**, located in Philadelphia's Independence Hall, got its **famous crack** during its first test.

STATE FACTS

Nickname: The Keystone State

State Capital: Harrisburg

Date of Statehood: December 12, 1787, the 2nd state

State Bird: Ruffed Grouse

State Mammal: White-Tailed Deer

State Flower: Mountain Laurel

RHODE ISLAND

Use your stickers to fill in Rhode Island's famous landmarks!

MASSACHUSETTS

Born in Providence, Rhode Island, in **1878**, **George M. Cohan** wrote the **PATRIOTIC SONGS** **"You're a Grand Old Flag"** and **"I'm a Yankee Doodle Dandy."**

In **1876**, **POLO** was played for the first time in the United States in Rhode Island.

America's **oldest CAROUSEL** is located in Watch Hill, Rhode Island.

CONNECTICUT

STATE FACTS

Nickname: The Ocean State

State Capital: Providence

Date of Statehood: May 29, 1790, the 13th state

State Bird: Rhode Island Red Chicken

State Flower: Violet

Rhode Island, located on the Atlantic Ocean in New England, is the smallest U.S. state. Rhode Island was the last of the thirteen original colonies to become a state. Rhode Island was the site of many battles from the American Revolution. Although small, Rhode Island played a major role in United States history.

Rhode Island
13th state
May 29, 1790

PROVIDENCE

Rhode Island is home to the **TENNIS HALL OF FAME**.

ATLANTIC OCEAN

Newport

Tennis Hall of Fame

The **first CIRCUS** in the United States was held in Newport, Rhode Island, in **1774**.

Watch Hill

SOUTH CAROLINA

Use your stickers to fill in South Carolina's famous landmarks!

NORTH CAROLINA

COLUMBIA

Bomb Island

Summerville

Morgan Island

GEORGIA

The **Spanish** brought **HOGS** to South Carolina in the **1500s**. They still freely roam the state today.

Each year, **thousands** of **PURPLE MARTINS**, the **largest swallows in North America**, roost on Bomb Island for the spring and summer.

Morgan Island is the only free-ranging colony of **MACAQUE MONKEYS**. Nearly **3,500 monkeys** live there.

South Carolina was one of the original thirteen colonies. The Civil War began at Fort Sumter in South Carolina in 1861. Today, South Carolina is known for its sprawling beaches and hundreds of golf courses, including the famous Myrtle Beach Golf Course.

South Carolina
8th state
May 23, 1788

There are around **300 GOLF COURSES** in South Carolina.

ATLANTIC OCEAN

Summerville, South Carolina, is the birthplace of **SWEET TEA**.

STATE FACTS

Nickname: The Palmetto State

State Capital: Columbia

Date of Statehood: May 23, 1788, the 8th state

State Bird: Carolina Wren

State Mammal: White-Tailed Deer

State Flower: Yellow Jessamine

SOUTH DAKOTA

Use your stickers to fill in South Dakota's famous landmarks!

NORTH DAKOTA

○ Sturgis

○ Black Hills

⭐ PIERRE

NEBRASKA

The **BLACK HILLS** in South Dakota are named from the Lakota phrase meaning **"hills that are black."** From a distance, the trees on the hills appear to be black.

Every year, **thousands of people** ride motorcycles to Sturgis, South Dakota, for the **country's largest MOTORCYCLE RALLY**.

CRAZY HORSE, the **Native American Ogala chief** who fought against the United States government, was born in South Dakota's Black Hills.

COLORADO

When President Thomas Jefferson doubled the size of the United States with the Louisiana Purchase, present-day South Dakota was part of the acquired land. South Dakota's landscape consists of fields and rolling hills. The major tourist attraction in South Dakota is Mount Rushmore—giant portraits of four U.S. presidents carved into a mountain. South Dakota has also been a rich site for uncovering many dinosaur and prehistoric fossils!

South Dakota
40th state
November 2, 1889

MINNESOTA

The best-preserved T.REX, named **Sue**, was uncovered in South Dakota in **1990**. Her skull was nearly **five feet long**!

South Dakota is home to the **Dakota, Lakota, and Nakota tribes** that make up the SIOUX NATION.

IOWA

STATE FACTS

Nickname: The Mount Rushmore State

State Capital: Pierre

Date of Statehood: November 2, 1889, the 40th state

State Bird: Chinese Ring-Necked Pheasant

State Mammal: Coyote

State Flower: Pasque flower

TENNESSEE

Use your stickers to fill in Tennessee's famous landmarks!

ILLINOIS

INDIANA

Reelfoot Lake in Tennessee is known as the **"TURTLE CAPITAL OF THE WORLD,"** and is home to **thousands of sliders, stinkpots, mud, and map turtles**.

A **replica** of **Greece's famous PARTHENON** is located in Centennial Park in Nashville.

KENTUCKY

MISSOURI

NASHVILLE

Reelfoot Lake

ARKANSAS

Memphis

ALABAMA

ELVIS PRESLEY's home, **Graceland**, is located in Memphis, Tennessee.

Tennessee has around **3,800** documented **CAVES** throughout the state.

MISSISSIPPI

Tennessee is a southern state named after a Cherokee village called Tanasi. One of the most visited parks in the world, Great Smoky Mountains National Park is situated in Tennessee and its neighbor, North Carolina. Tennessee is also a very musical state; it's the birthplace of both country and bluegrass!

Tennessee
16th state
June 1, 1796

OHIO

WEST VIRGINIA

NORTH CAROLINA

SOUTH CAROLINA

GEORGIA

Smoky Mountains National Park

Known as the **"salamander capital of the world,"** more than **thirty types** of SALAMANDERS are found in Smoky Mountains National Park.

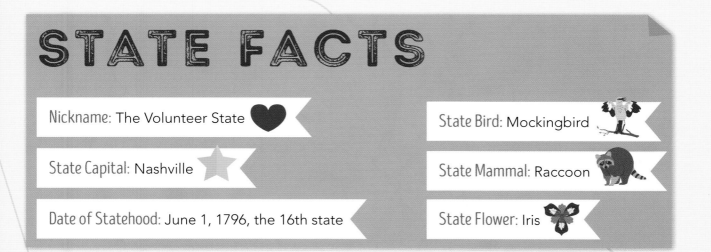

STATE FACTS

Nickname: The Volunteer State

State Capital: Nashville

Date of Statehood: June 1, 1796, the 16th state

State Bird: Mockingbird

State Mammal: Raccoon

State Flower: Iris

TEXAS

Use your stickers to fill in Texas's famous landmarks!

At **Dinosaur Valley State Park** in Texas, you can find and follow real **DINOSAUR FOOTPRINTS** that are millions of years old!

More land is farmed in **TEXAS** than in any other state.

OKLAHOMA

NEW MEXICO

Dinosaur Valley State Park ◯

MEXICO

☆
AUSTIN

There are about **16 million CATTLE** in the state of Texas.

There are **more species of BATS** in Texas than in any other state.

Known as the "Lone Star State," Texas is the second-largest state in the U.S. Located along the Gulf of Mexico, Texas is home to cattle, barbecue, and the famous Battle of the Alamo. A special symbol for Texans, the Alamo, played a major role in the battle for independence from Mexico.

Texas
28th state
December 29, 1845

The first word spoken from the Moon during **APOLLO 11** on **July 20, 1969**, was **"Houston,"** the city where the mission control was located.

Houston

STATE FACTS

Nickname: The Lone Star State ★

State Capital: Austin ★

Date of Statehood: December 29, 1845, the 28th state

State Bird: Mockingbird

State Mammals: Texas Longhorn and Nine-Banded Armadillo

State Flower: Bluebonnet

UTAH

Use your stickers to fill in Utah's famous landmarks!

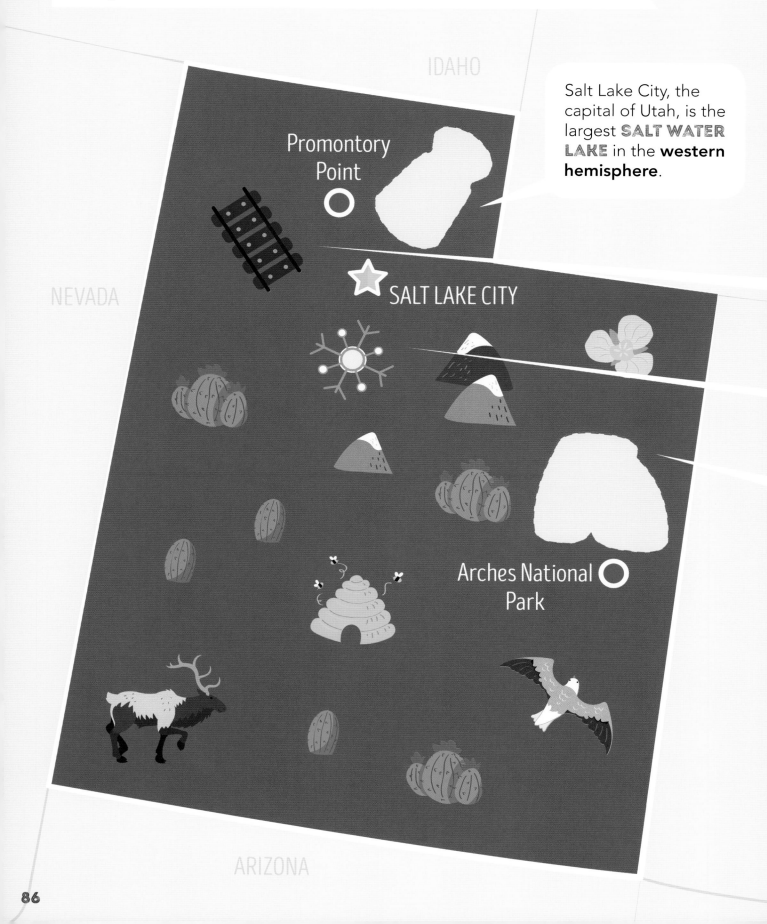

Salt Lake City, the capital of Utah, is the largest **SALT WATER LAKE** in the **western hemisphere**.

IDAHO

Promontory Point

SALT LAKE CITY

NEVADA

Arches National Park

ARIZONA

WYOMING

From the Native American word meaning "people of the mountains," Utah was the 45th state. Utah is made up of deserts, mountains, and plateaus. One of the most popular destinations in Utah, Arches National Park is home to thousands of natural rock arches.

Utah
45th state
January 4, 1896

The first **TRANSCONTINENTAL RAILROAD** was completed at Promontory Point in **1869**.

The mountains around Salt Lake City receive around **500 inches** of **SNOW** a year!

Arches National Park in Moab has more than 2,000 natural stone arches. **RAINBOW BRIDGE** in **Lake Powell** is the **biggest natural bridge** in the world.

COLORADO

STATE FACTS

Nickname: The Beehive State

State Capital: Salt Lake City

Date of Statehood: January 4, 1896, the 45th state

State Bird: California Seagull

State Mammal: Rocky Mountain Elk

State Flower: Sego Lily

VERMONT

Use your stickers to fill in Vermont's famous landmarks!

CANADA

Jericho

MONTPELIER

Wilson "Snowflake" Bentley photographed over **5,000** SNOWFLAKES in Jericho, Vermont, and learned that **no two snowflakes are alike**.

NEW HAMPSHIRE

NEW YORK

Ben and Jerry's ICE CREAM began in Vermont.

Brattleboro

MASSACHUSETTS

Vermont, located in the northeast, is a small state that is only 160 miles long and 80 miles wide. It is covered in forest and is a popular destination in the winter for skiers and snowboarders. Vermont is known for its beautiful landscapes, and of course, maple syrup!

Vermont
14th state
March 4, 1791

MAINE

Vermont produces over **500,000 gallons** of MAPLE SYRUP a year, more than any other state.

ATLANTIC OCEAN

RUDYARD KIPLING, the author of **The Jungle Book**, lived in Brattleboro, Vermont.

STATE FACTS

Nickname: The Green Mountain State

State Capital: Montpelier

Date of Statehood: March 4, 1791, the 14th state

State Bird: Hermit Thrush

State Mammal: Morgan Horse

State Flower: Red Clover

VIRGINIA

Use your stickers to fill in Virginia's famous landmarks!

OHIO

PENNSYLVANIA

WEST VIRGINIA

America's first president **George Washington**'s house, MOUNT VERNON, is located in Virginia.

Thomas Jefferson built his home, MONTICELLO, in Virginia.

KENTUCKY

RICHMOND

NORTH CAROLINA

TENNESSEE

STATE FACTS

Nickname: The Old Dominion State

State Capital: Richmond

Date of Statehood: June 25, 1788, the 10th state

State Bird: Cardinal

State Flower: Dogwood

GEORGIA

SOUTH CAROLINA

Virginia, one of the original thirteen colonies, played an important role in American history. The early colonists settled in Virginia and later the state was the site for major battles in the American Revolution and Civil War. Virginia was also the birthplace for two of America's founding fathers, George Washington and Thomas Jefferson.

Virginia
10th state
June 25, 1788

● Assateague Island

WILD PONIES have grazed on Assateague Island for **centuries**.

Virginia was named after England's QUEEN ELIZABETH I, known as the **"Virgin Queen."**

Virginia was the **first state** to grow PEANUTS in the United States.

ATLANTIC OCEAN

WASHINGTON

Use your stickers to fill in Washington's famous landmarks!

Native Americans who lived in the Pacific Northwest are known for their **TOTEM POLES**, giant carvings made from a single large tree. The **carvings of animals** and other objects have special meanings.

PACIFIC OCEAN

ORCAS are the **official state marine mammal** of Washington. Orcas rely on their **highly developed vocalizations** and hearing ability for navigating, finding prey, and communication.

Seattle

OLYMPIA

OREGON

STATE FACTS

Nickname: The Evergreen State

State Capital: Olympia

Date of Statehood: November 11, 1889, the 42nd state

State Bird: Willow Goldfinch

State Marine Mammal: Orca Whale

State Flower: Coast Rhododendron

CANADA

Washington, "the Evergreen State," is the only state that is named after a president. The 42nd state was named after our first president, George Washington. It is located in the Pacific Northwest region of the United States, south of the Canadian province of British Columbia. Washington is home to lush, green forests, rivers and lakes, and volcanoes!

Washington
42nd State
November 11th, 1889

The **SPACE NEEDLE** in Seattle was built for the **1962 World's Fair** and is **605 feet tall**. When it was built, it was the tallest structure west of the Mississippi River.

IDAHO

MONTANA

Washington is home to **five major volcanoes**. In 1980, the volcano **MOUNT ST. HELENS** erupted for 9 hours! Nearly 150 square miles of forest were devastated.

APPLES are the largest agricultural product grown in Washington State. Each year **10-12 billion apples** are handpicked in Washington.

WEST VIRGINIA

Use your stickers to fill in West Virginia's famous landmarks!

The first **SODA MACHINE** was patented in **1833** in Wheeling, West Virginia.

West Virginia is nearly all forest. Around **75 percent** of the state is covered with **TREES**.

PENNSYLVANIA

OHIO

Wheeling

Soda

CHARLESTON

KENTUCKY

The first **STEAMBOAT** was launched from West Virginia in **1787** on the **Potomac River**.

VIRGINIA

STATE FACTS

Nickname: The Mountain State

State Capital: Charleston

Date of Statehood: June 20, 1863, the 35th state

State Bird: Cardinal

State Mammal: Black Bear

State Flower: Rhododendron

NORTH CAROLINA

WISCONSIN

Use your stickers to fill in Wisconsin's famous landmarks!

LAKE SUPERIOR

Wisconsin is the **DAIRY** capital of the United States; it produces more **milk** than any other state.

The **famous magician HARRY HOUDINI** was from Wisconsin.

MICHIGAN

MINNESOTA

Famous American **architect FRANK LLOYD WRIGHT** was born in Richland Center, Wisconsin.

Wisconsin is the nation's leader in dairy production. In fact, some Wisconsin natives even refer to themselves as "cheese heads"! Wisconsin was an important stop on the Underground Railroad— slaves passed through there to gain freedom in Canada.

Wisconsin 30th state May 29, 1848

Richland Center

MADISON

ILLINOIS

STATE FACTS

Nickname: The Badger State

State Capital: Madison

Date of Statehood: May 29, 1848, the 30th state

State Bird: American Robin

State Mammal: Badger

State Flower: Wood Violet

MISSOURI

WYOMING

Use your stickers to fill in Wyoming's famous landmarks!

Wyoming was the **first state** to give **women** the **RIGHT TO VOTE**.

MONTANA

Yellowstone became the **first national park** in the nation in **1872**. It's the home of **OLD FAITHFUL**, a famous **geyser** that erupts about every **91 minutes**.

Yellowstone National Park

UTAH

Kemmerer

CHEYENNE

Although it's one of the largest U.S. states, Wyoming has the smallest population. It is home to a wide variety of wildlife, including one of the most popular national parks: Yellowstone. Whether it's Old Faithful, Devils Tower, or animals such as wolves and bears, Wyoming has something for everyone.

Wyoming
44th state
July 10, 1890

Over 100,000 **FISH FOSSILS** have been found in Kemmerer, Wyoming.

COLORADO

STATE FACTS

Nickname: The Equality State

State Capital: Cheyenne

Date of Statehood: July 10, 1890, the 44th state

State Bird: Meadowlark

State Mammal: Bison

State Flower: Indian Paintbrush